THE BEGINNER'S
Cursive
HANDWRITING WORKBOOK

THE BEGINNER'S

Cursive

HANDWRITING WORKBOOK

Learn to Write Cursive with Wacky Jokes & Puzzles

CONNIE SLONE

IMPORTANCE OF CURSIVE WRITING

Cursive is more than the next level of handwriting. It's a way to improve yourself and be creative. The exercises in this workbook train your hands to move more easily, strengthening your coordination. Did you know cursive can help you remember things too?

Connecting letters (smoothly) means writing faster while making your handwriting look beautiful. Plus, learning cursive is something to feel proud of because not everyone can do it well. Even though we use computers a lot these days, learning to write in cursive is still important, and many schools want you to learn it.

BENEFITS OF LEARNING CURSIVE

Studies show learning cursive helps your brain grow. This type of writing improves your memory and helps your brain hold onto the things you write down. And since you'll develop control, writing in a smooth, thoughtful way, your overall hand–eye coordination will improve! Writing in cursive often helps you read better too!

Why? Because cursive writing uses important parts of your brain that help you understand words. Practicing cursive helps your brain develop in a way that is unique.

HOW TO USE THIS WORKBOOK

START BY TRACING LETTERS: In the beginning, you will trace over the lines to learn how each letter should look. This will help you get used to the shapes and movements of cursive writing.

WRITE BY YOURSELF: After you trace your letters, the tracing exercises will include blank lines for you to practice writing on your own.

TAKE ON CHALLENGES AS YOU LEARN: As you improve, there will be less tracing and more writing on your own. This will help you become even better at cursive.

HAVE FUN WITH ACTIVITIES: To keep things fun, this workbook has puzzles, jokes, and creative prompts to enjoy while you practice.

COMPLETE YOUR FINAL GOALS: At the end, you'll be able to write whole paragraphs and even create your own cursive project. Don't forget to get your certificate and show off your new skills!

PROPER HAND AND PENCIL POSITION

To write in cursive, it's important to sit comfortably and hold your pencil the right way. Sit up straight with both feet on the floor. Hold your pencil between your thumb and your first two fingers (gently, not too tight). Rest your arm on the table so you can move your hand smoothly across the page. Keep the paper at a slight angle, so your arm can follow the lines easily. Good posture and a relaxed grip will make writing in cursive much easier!

Now, get yourself into position! Remember to:

SIT UP STRAIGHT, FEET FLAT

HOLD PENCIL WITH THUMB AND FIRST TWO FINGERS

REST ARM ON THE TABLE

ANGLE PAPER SLIGHTLY

EXPLANATION OF THE CURSIVE ALPHABET

Cursive is about connecting each of the letters in a word. That means each letter is drawn in a way to connect to one another. Cursive writing is often faster and feels more natural (kind of like drawing) because it's made to flow. Imagine you're drawing a line that doesn't stop until the whole word is done. The more you practice, the more you'll see how the letters connect and make your writing special.

You'll notice many of the letters look familiar since they're very similar to the print version of the letter. Other letters are very different (just take a look at the letter "q" or "z"). These letters may require more practice, but don't worry.

All of the cursive letter exercises in this workbook show you exactly how to draw each letter—uppercase and lowercase—step by step!

LETTERS A-Z LOWERCASE:

For your first exercise, you'll begin by writing all the lowercase letters in cursive. Each letter is made to fit together easily with the next one, helping your words flow. First, trace over the dotted lines to get used to the movement. It might feel a little strange at first (like learning to ride a bike). That's totally normal! Just keep practicing, and soon it will feel easier. Follow the arrows to know where to move your pencil. Think of each letter as a link in a chain—when they all connect, they make words!

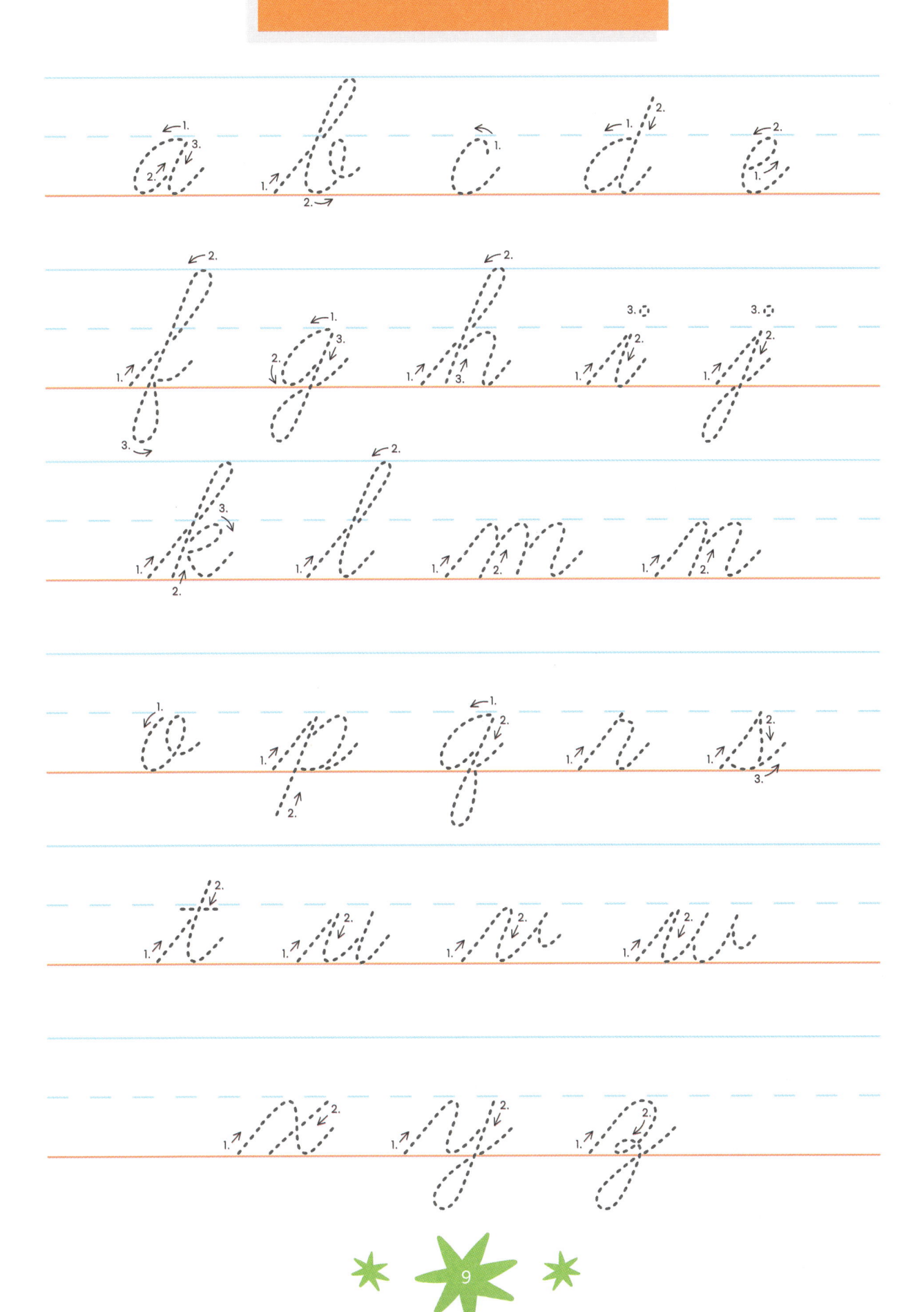

LETTERS A-Z UPPERCASE:

Now it's time for you to practice all the cursive uppercase letters. These letters are larger and can sometimes look different from the lowercase version. Begin by tracing the dotted lines, following the arrows. Uppercase letters are often the first letter of names or sentences, so it's important to make them stand out (especially when writing your own name). That means they'll take up the full height of your line of paper.

Important: Don't rush—follow the arrows carefully and take your time. Each uppercase letter is unique, almost like its own little piece of art. With some practice, you'll be writing each uppercase letter like a pro!

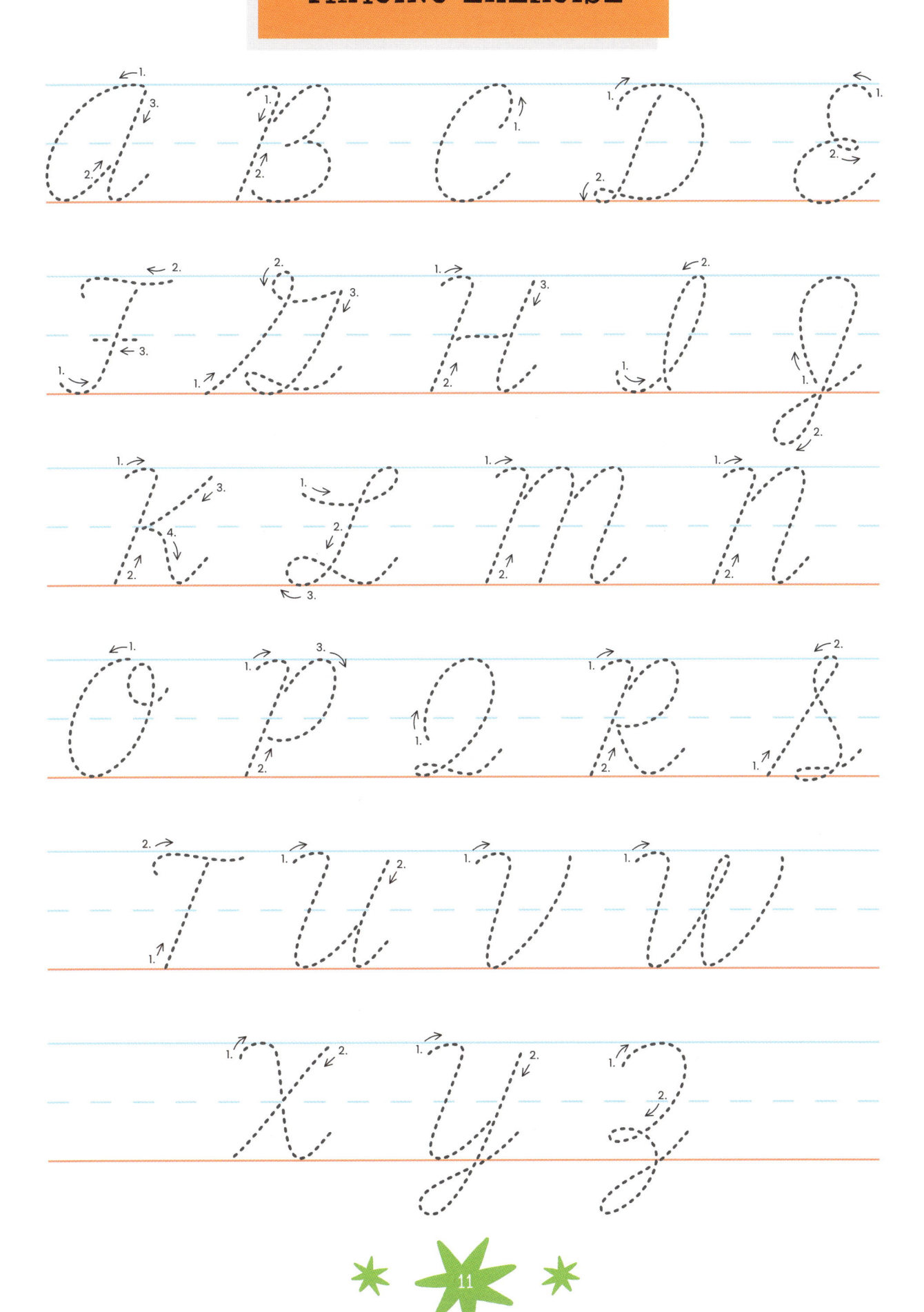

11

COMMON LETTER COMBINATIONS:

Let's move on to cursive "letter joins"! In this section, you'll learn to write some of the most common letter pairs found in everyday words, like "nd" for example. These two letters are in so many words, like "and," "land," "sand". . . Can you think of any others?

These letter joins are the first steps to writing full words in cursive, helping you connect letters smoothly and confidently. Start by tracing the dotted pairs to see how they link together. It might feel different at first since this is where you really start seeing how cursive letters flow into one another. Take your time, follow the arrows, and soon you'll be joining letters like a pro!

th he in er an

re on at en nd

ti es or te of

ed is it al ar

st to nt ha as

io le ve co me

de hi se ma el

ro di no ha us

SIMPLE WORDS FOR TRACING

Now that you've practiced letters (both uppercase and lowercase) and put together those common pairs (letter joins)—it's time to trace full words!

In this exercise, you'll see common words you probably use all the time. Each word starts with dotted tracing lines to help guide you. After that, use the blank section of the line to write the word on your own. Take your time and focus on keeping all the letters connected smoothly. Tracing and then writing helps you remember the shapes and makes your handwriting even better. Keep practicing, and soon you'll be writing these words with no problem at all!

and the cat dog

bat red sun can

hat big run bed

cup pen pot rat

map fan cow sky

box top net fox

leg tin hop bug

rug pig job tag

van lip fit jet

mat kit nut zip

book play hand

feet jump frog

tree moon star

blue fish bird

snow wind hill

sand ship boat

fire wood door

home cake ball

rock milk desk

lamp roof park

game ring sing

frog milk food

seed shop

road tent

FUN, KID-FRIENDLY WORDS FOR PRACTICE

In this section, it's all about writing some of your favorite words! You'll get to trace and write words that you hear or use every day. These words are meant to be playful and easy, like "magic," "jump," and "pizza"—words that make you smile! Each word has a few tracing lines to help guide you, followed by blank lines for you to try writing them on your own.

When tracing, pay close attention to how the letters connect. Cursive is all about keeping each word flowing fluidly, like a wave. Once you feel comfortable, use the blank lines to try writing the words without any guides. It might be tricky at first, but with practice, you'll notice it gets easier and your writing becomes more confident.

Don't worry if your letters don't look perfect right away. The key is to have fun while you practice! Think of it as drawing each word, making sure your pencil moves smoothly and connects all the letters just like a chain. Before long, you'll be able to write all kinds of fun words in cursive!

magic jump pizza

rainbow giggle

happy smile sparkle

sunshine rocket apple

banana tiger ocean

bubbles popcorn

dance monkey hero

cupcake adventure

dream candy fairy

cookie explore kitten

puppy guitar whistle

flower castle balloon

dragon adventure

laugh music swing

skateboard crayons

friends story race

chocolate butterfly

surprise star cloud

rainbow treasure

carousel unicorn

27

SHORT SENTENCES FOR PRACTICE

Now it's time to practice writing some short sentences in cursive! These sentences are simple and fun, using many of the words you've already practiced. Start by tracing over the dotted lines to get comfortable with how each word connects in a sentence. After that, use the blank lines to write the sentences on your own.

Remember to keep your letters connected and flowing smoothly, just like you did with individual words. Don't worry if it feels challenging at first—every sentence you write will make you better at cursive. Have fun, and enjoy seeing your words turn into full sentences in beautiful handwriting!

The quick fox jumped over

the lazy dog.

Zoe loves to explore

magical forests.

Giraffes eat leaves

from tall trees.

Bobby can bake a

yummy chocolate cake.

The kitten played with
a bright red ball.

I saw a rainbow
after the rain.

31

The wind carried the

blue kite high.

Lucy and Max found

a hidden treasure.

Elephants splash water

with their trunks.

Tommy likes to ride

his green bike.

Jelly beans come in
many fun colors.

The bright moon lit up
the night sky.

Sarah can whistle

a happy tune.

The puppy dug a hole

in the garden.

Alex brought cookies

to share at school.

The dragon flew over

the castle.

Xander found a shiny
seashell on the shore.

My friends and I love
to play outside.

Yellow flowers bloom

in the springtime.

Vicky saw a zebra at

the zoo yesterday.

The garden is full of
buzzing bees.

Penny found a
four-leaf clover.

The friendly dog

wagged its tail.

My brother plays

with a toy robot.

The owl hooted softly

in the night.

I like to draw pictures

with crayons.

The squirrel ran up

the tall tree.

Kayla made a necklace

from shells.

The stars twinkled in
the clear sky.

Grandpa tells the best
bedtime stories.

The car zoomed down

the windy road.

An eagle soared above

the mountains.

We picked apples from
the orchard.

The candles glowed on
the birthday cake.

Jake and Lily built

a sandcastle.

The rabbit hopped

through the field.

Mom made a tasty
fruit salad.

The blue jay sang in
the morning.

Dinosaurs roamed the

Earth long ago.

The ice cream melted

in the sun.

NAMES AND PLACES

This section will help you practice writing names and places in cursive! You'll trace names of people and places you might know, like "George Washington," "New York City," and "London, England." These are words you might see often, and learning to write them beautifully will make your cursive even more special.

Each name or place starts with tracing lines to help you get the hang of it, followed by blank lines for practice. Pay attention to how capital letters stand out from the rest of the word. With practice, you'll be able to write names and places in cursive!

George Washington

Harriet Tubman

Abraham Lincoln

Helen Keller

Rosa Parks

Alexander Graham Bell

Amelia Earhart

Benjamin Franklin

Martin Luther King Jr.

Neil Armstrong

Sacagawea

Thomas Edison

Pocahontas

Susan B. Anthony

Anne Frank

Harriet Beecher Stowe

John F. Kennedy

Cleopatra

Leonardo da Vinci

Walt Disney

New York City

Mount Rushmore

Statue of Liberty

Grand Canyon

Taj Mahal

Washington, D.C.

Golden Gate Bridge

Eiffel Tower

Great Wall of China

Niagara Falls

London, England

Sydney Opera House

Pyramids of Giza

Mount Everest

Big Ben

Coloseum

Amazon Rainforest

Rome, Italy

Mount Fuji

Paris, France

EVERYDAY CURSIVE SCENARIOS

Cursive writing isn't only for school. Once you learn the basics, connecting your letters helps you in everyday life too! On the next pages, you'll see five common exercises people use cursive for all the time.

EXERCISE 1

GROCERY LIST

Writing a grocery list is a great way to practice cursive in an everyday context! We'll start with simple items and move on to some that are a little more challenging. Trace and copy the first three words, then write the next three words in cursive. Finally, use the hints to figure out what food item to write out in cursive!

milk bread eggs

carrots apples cheese

I am a leafy green, often
found in salads.

I am red, round, and
used in ketchup.

I am really good
in guacamole.

I am a long yellow fruit
that grows on trees.

WRITE A CHECK

Writing a check is another real-world skill where cursive is important! In this exercise, you'll be writing a check to a fictional zoo.

The name of the zoo will be written in traceable cursive letters for you to practice, and the numerical dollar amount will already be filled out. You'll then trace the written dollar amount in cursive to match the numbers. Finally, there's a blank spot for your signature— try your best to create your own unique signature here!

PAY TO THE ORDER OF *Happy Valley Zoo*

$ 25.00

Twenty-five DOLLARS

SIGNATURE

FILL OUT AN ENVELOPE

Learning to fill out an envelope is a useful skill that helps you send letters to friends and family! In this exercise, you'll practice writing the address in cursive. You'll trace the recipient's name and address in cursive, while the return address will be written by you.

The recipient's name and address are provided in traceable cursive letters for you to practice. The return address section is blank, giving you the opportunity to write your own name and address. Make sure to keep all letters flowing smoothly and pay attention to spacing!

John Smith

123 Main Street

Springfield, USA 45678

TO-DO LIST

Creating a to-do list is another practical way to use cursive every day! In this exercise, you'll write out tasks to help organize your day. The first three items are traceable, the next three are in print for you to write in cursive, and the last three are left blank for you to come up with your own tasks!

Feed the cat

Clean your room

Do homework

Walk the dog

Water the plants

Pack lunch

LABELING SCHOOL SUPPLIES

In this exercise, you'll practice labeling common school supplies in cursive. You'll see 8–10 outline drawings of different items, like folders, coloring pencils, and notebooks. Two of these items have labels in traceable cursive for you to follow. The rest are blank, allowing you to fill in the correct label or make up your own name for the item. Feel free to get creative while practicing your cursive skills!

Remember to keep your letters flowing smoothly and neatly as you fill in the labels. Have fun with the names you choose!

pencil

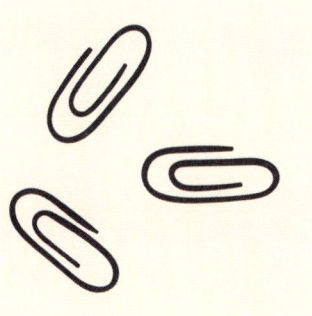

protractor

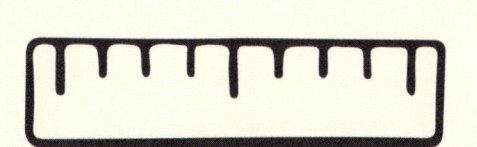

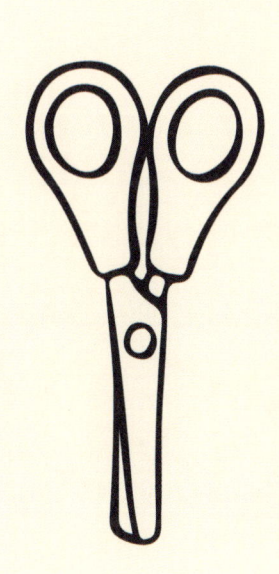

100 JOKES IN CURSIVE WRITING!

Get ready for some fun while practicing your cursive! In this section, you'll work with jokes that will make you smile while improving your handwriting. Some of the jokes will have traceable words for both the question and the answer. Other jokes will have answers in print for you to write in cursive. It's a mix of tracing and writing on your own—a great way to sharpen your cursive skills while having a good laugh!

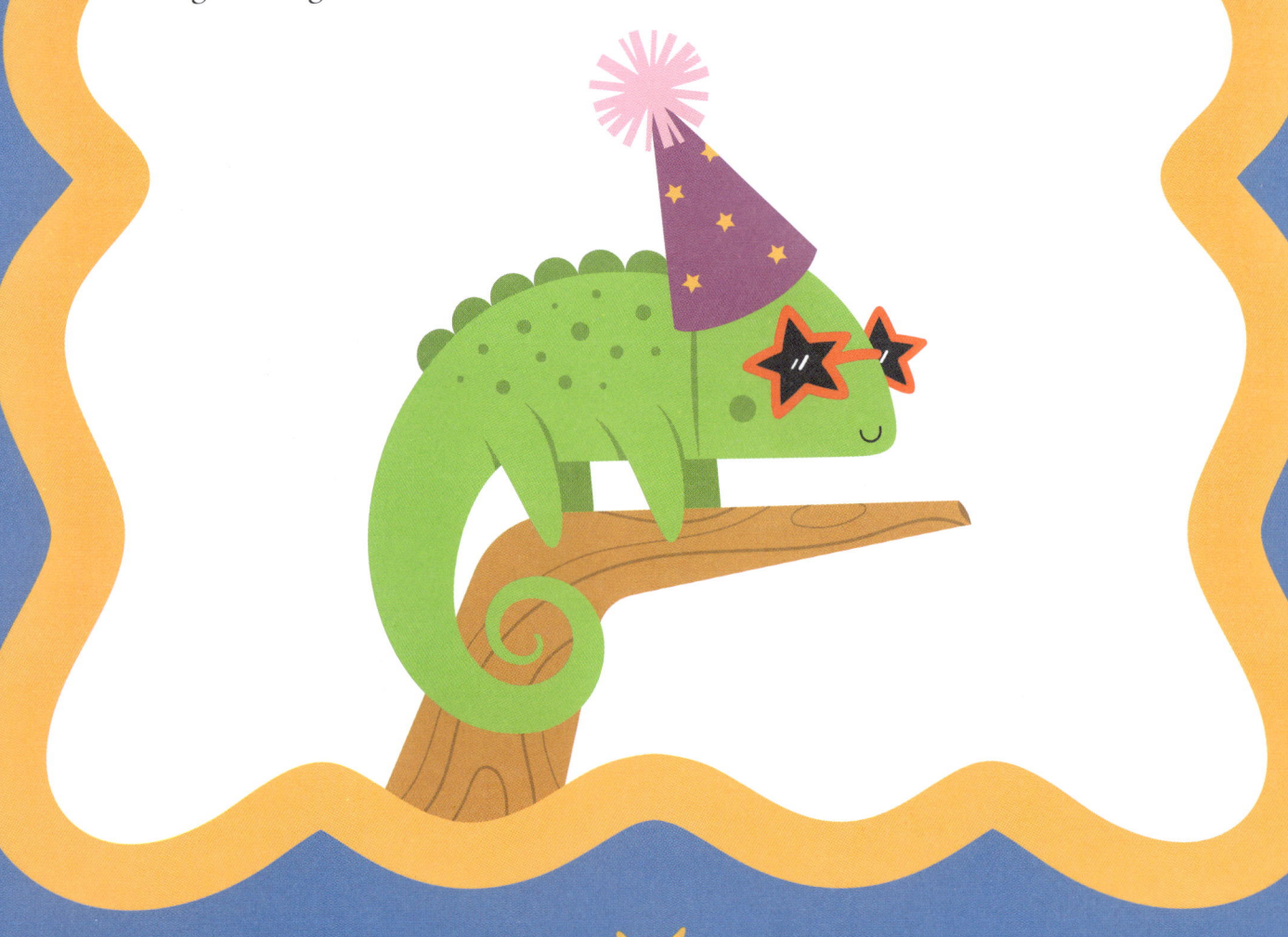

ANIMAL JOKES

Why do chameleons make great party guests?
They always blend in.

Why was the lion sad and lonely?

He had no pride.

What do you get if you cross an antelope with a journalist?
A gnus reporter.

What do you get if you cross a
skunk with a hand grenade?
A stink bomb.

What's black and white and
slowly turning blue?

A very cold penguin.

What happens when two zebras
crash into each other?
They see stars and stripes.

What do you call a ram that lives at the top of a mountain?
A hillbilly goat.

What do you get when you cross a kangaroo with a jungle vine?

A jump rope.

What do you get if you cross a sheep and a large primate?
A bah-boon.

What do you get if you cross
frogs with chameleons?

Leapin' lizards.

What's black and white
and green all over?

A sloppy skunk eating pea soup.

What do you get if you cross a
hyena and a parrot?

An animal that laughs and
then asks itself what's so funny.

ANIMAL JOKES

What kind of sharks

live in the desert?

Sand sharks.

What's soggy and has

large antlers?

A rain deer.

Why couldn't the herd of deer

buy dinner?

Because they only had

one buck.

Did you hear the owl's
new joke?
It was a hoot.

How do you get rid of
unwanted rabbits?

Use hare remover.

What do you call a boy slug
that lives in a shell?
Snail male.

What do you get if you cross a rabbit with morning mist?

Hare spray.

What is a squirrel's favorite Christmas show?

The Nutcracker.

What happened to the frog that parked near a fire hydrant?

He got toad away.

How do rabbits fly to Europe?
They take a hare plane.

What is a skunk's
favorite holiday?

Scent Valentine's Day.

What do you get if you
cross an Australian animal
with a cheerleader?
A kangarooter.

Do rabbits use combs?

No. They use hare brushes.

What do you call a pig

who does karate?

Pork chop.

What goes bounce! Bonk!

Bounce! Bonk! Bounce! Bonk?

A kangaroo hopping around

in a room with a low ceiling.

Did you hear the pig joke?

It was boar-ing.

What kind of sharks eat lions?

Mane-eaters.

What do you call a cow
without legs?
Ground beef.

Where do cows go for fun?
To the moo-vies.

What do you call a fish's dad?

The cod father.

Father: Stop misbehaving and I'll tell you the joke about the big Christmas present.

Boy: And if I don't stop misbehaving?

Father: Then you won't get it.

What did the calf say
to the silo?

Is my fodder in there?

My wife refuses to go to
karaoke with me.

I have to duet alone.

Why are rich Englishmen
so strong?

All their money is
measured in pounds.

FAMILY JOKES

My archaeologist friend has
been depressed lately.
His life is really in ruins.

I swapped my bed for a
trampoline.

My wife hit the roof.

What did the dad
who bought his son a fridge
for Christmas say?
I hope you like it, it's cool.

MEDICAL JOKES

Patient: Doc, am I really as
ugly as people say I am?
Psychologist: Of course not.
Patient: Then why did
you make me lie face down
on your couch?

What does a sick lemon say?

I'm feeling sour.

MEDICAL JOKES

What is a podiatrist's favorite TV game show?

Heel of fortune.

Patient: Did you hear what I told you? I said I'm as sick as a dog! Doctor: Stop barking at me and sit down.

MEDICAL JOKES

Patient: Help me, doctor! I just swallowed my harmonica.

Doctor: Luckily you don't play the piano.

Why did the window shade go to the psychologist?

It was uptight.

Where do phlebotomists go to college?

IV league schools.

Why did Santa Claus go to a psychologist?

Because he didn't believe in himself.

What did the arm bone say to the funny bone?

You're quite humerus.

Why do dentists never lie?

They value the tooth at any cost.

Why are there always openings at a dentist's office?

They're always looking to fill holes.

Why was the old house crying?

It had window pains.

Boy: If you broke your arm in two places, what would you do?

Girl: Stay out of those two places.

MEDICAL JOKES

Why did the werewolf go
to the psychologist?
He had a hair-raising
experience.

What do you get if you cross
a star and a podiatrist?

Twinkle toes.

Patient: Help me, doctor!
I think I'm a deck of cards!
Doctor: I'll deal with you later.

Why do podiatrists always lose?

All they ever see is de-feet.

Man: Every time I travel on
a plane, I get sick.
Doctor: It sounds like you
have the flew.

Why do doctors make
good parents?

They have plenty of patients.

Did you hear about the boy who wanted to be a dentist? He was enameled by the profession.

Did you hear about the mean dentist?

He hurts your fillings.

Did you hear the balloon joke?

It's a bit long-winded.

Did you hear about the

theater show about puns?

It was a play on words.

Did you hear about

the guy who invented the

knock-knock joke?

He won the no-bell prize.

Why was the sink so tired?

It was feeling drained.

Did you hear about the pencil

with two erasers?

It was pointless.

Did you hear about

the butter rumor?

You probably shouldn't

spread it.

Did you hear about the child who wouldn't take a nap?

He was resisting a rest.

Did you hear about the rowboat sale?

It's an oar-deal.

Did you hear about the man who sued the airline for misplacing his luggage?

He lost his case.

MISCELLANEOUS JOKES

Did you hear about the restaurant on the moon? Great food, but no atmosphere.

Did you hear about the funny sea monster?

He's Kraken me up.

What do you call a place where they make things that are just okay? A satisfactory.

MISCELLANEOUS JOKES

What do you call a pen
without a top?
De-cap-itated.

What do you call a
chicken's ghost?

A poultrygeist.

Did you hear the joke
about the omelet?
It was eggcellent.

94

Why did the playing card
become a ship?

It wanted to be a full deck.

What do you call a horse
who disagrees with you?

A neigh-sayer.

Why was the campsite
always stressed?

Everything was two in tents.

Why did the bulletin board

quit his job?

He just couldn't tack

it anymore.

What do you call a

lazy kangaroo?

A pouch potato.

Why did the shoe go to heaven?

It had a good sole.

Why did the wheel

get an education?

Because it wanted to

be well-rounded.

Why did the chef put a

clock in a hot pan?

He wanted to see time fry.

Why do cakes smell so good?

They have a lot of flower.

MISCELLANEOUS JOKES

Why did the referee get
a new phone?

Because he kept missing calls.

Why did the family
sell their vacuum?

It was just collecting dust.

Why did the man
accidentally call the hole
in the ground a sewer?

He meant well.

MISCELLANEOUS JOKES

Why did the cookie
go to the doctor?
Because he felt crummy.

Why do the numbers 1 to 12
work the hardest?

They're on the clock.

Why was the philosopher
so busy?
Because he had a lot
on his Plato.

Why did the man get fired from

the calendar factory?

He took a couple days off.

Why was the ocean

being investigated?

Because it was a bit fishy.

Why did rearranging the

furniture help the restaurant?

Because now the tables

have turned.

MISCELLANEOUS JOKES

Why are concert halls so cold?

Because they're usually

full of fans.

Why couldn't the photographer

take a picture of the fog?

He mist his chance.

Why shouldn't you

believe an atom?

Because they make

up everything.

Why do eggs love these puns?

They crack them up.

Why should you always wash

a cheese slicer after using it?

For the grater good.

Why don't trees exercise?

Working out saps their strength.

Why did the gym close down?

It wasn't working out.

CURSIVE PUZZLES AND EXERCISES

You've come so far! Now it's time to turn up the fun and do some puzzles and creative art using cursive writing. In addition to writing words and phrases, you'll have to figure out backward words, come up with crossword answers, decipher codes in script, and even solve a cursive maze. Enjoy!

cup + *cake* = **?**

MIRROR WRITING FUN

Below are 10 words written in backwards cursive. Your challenge is to carefully copy each word in its correct form on the blank line provided next to it. Think about each letter and how it would look when reversed, then write it properly in cursive on the line.

CONNECT THE WORDS

Below are ten two-syllable words split into parts. Your task is to read each word part in the first two columns and then write the full word in cursive on the blank line provided in the third column. Focus on joining the two parts smoothly and making your letters flow together!

de cided _____

un done _____

for get _____

re member _____

mis take _____

sun set _____

cup cake _____

in vent _____

bed time _____

hap py _____

CURSIVE CROSSWORD PUZZLE

Below are clues for a crossword puzzle. Read each clue and write the answer in cursive in the crossword grid. Make sure to write each letter carefully and clearly so that your cursive is easy to read.

DOWN

1. Opposite of cold
3. A fruit that is red and often given to teachers
5. A farm animal that gives milk
6. The season after winter
7. A large body of water

ACROSS

1. Something you wear on your head
2. An animal that hops
4. Something you use to write
6. A place where you learn
8. Opposite of night

CURSIVE MAZE CHALLENGE

Below is a maze with different paths. Your task is to trace the correct path that will lead you to the end of the maze. When you finish tracing, you will see that your pencil path forms a fun, athletic-themed phrase written in cursive!

WORD ART DOODLE

Below are four words. Write each word in cursive and use your creativity to turn it into a piece of art by adding doodles around it. For example, you could draw decorations that relate to the word's meaning. Let your imagination run wild!

rainbow

sunshine

music

mountain

WORD SEARCH IN CURSIVE

Below is a word search filled with ten cursive words. All the words are related to a party theme! Your task is to find each word in the grid and highlight it. Then, write each word you find, in cursive, on the lines provided.

```
D  T  P  G  K  K  O  H  G  M
A  J  F  R  K  J  P  P  G  U
N  F  R  I  E  N  D  S  A  S
C  C  F  C  G  S  G  Z  M  I
I  A  U  E  A  I  E  S  E  C
N  K  J  V  S  N  I  N  S  X
G  E  O  X  A  W  D  R  T  R
S  N  A  C  K  S  B  L  B  S
U  P  A  R  T  Y  G  Y  E  R
B  A  L  L  O  O  N  S  M  S
```

SECRET CURSIVE MESSAGE

Below is a secret message written in cursive, but some of the letters are missing. Use the key at the top of the page to fill in the blanks and reveal the secret message. Make sure to write each letter carefully in cursive to complete the message.

KEY:

A = @
E = #
I = *
O = &
U = $

SECRET MESSAGE:

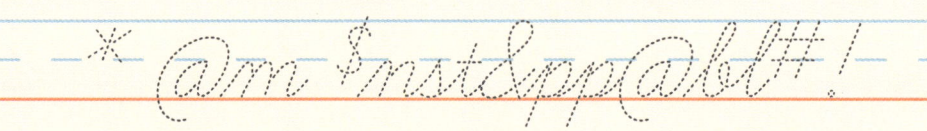

DECODED MESSAGE:

ANIMAL NAME CHALLENGE

Below are four animal names. Write each name in cursive and then draw a small picture of each animal next to the word. Use your imagination and have fun with the drawings!

elephant

giraffe

dolphin

kangaroo

FUN CURSIVE PROMPTS

So far, you have written and traced. Now it's time to take control and write what you have to say. On the following pages, there are three types of prompts, with four prompts of each type: imaginary journal entries, short story prompts, and prompts for notes and letters. Be as creative as you'd like in every scenario!

PROMPT 1

Write a journal entry as an adventurer who just found a mysterious map in the forest. What does it look like? What could it lead to?

PROMPT 2

Imagine you are a pirate who discovered a hidden treasure chest. What's inside it?

PROMPT 3

Pretend to be a scientist who just invented a new type of candy. What does it taste like and how did you create it?

PROMPT 4

You are an astronaut who just landed on a new planet. Write about what you see and the strange creatures you meet.

PROMPT 1

Write a story about a talking animal who goes on an adventure to find its long-lost friend.

PROMPT 2

Imagine there is a secret door in your classroom that leads somewhere amazing. Describe what happens when you open it.

PROMPT 3

Write a story about a magic pencil that brings drawings to life. What do you draw first?

PROMPT 4

Tell a story about a day when all the toys in your room come alive. What do they do?

PROMPT 1

Write a thank-you note to a friend who helped you when you were feeling sad.

PROMPT 2

Write a thank-you letter to a teacher who made learning fun for you.

PROMPT 3

Write a thank-you note to your parents or guardians for a special gift or surprise they gave you.

PROMPT 4

Write a letter to your favorite book character thanking them for their adventure.

FINAL CHALLENGE: CURSIVE REFLECTION

WOW, YOU'VE MADE IT TO THE FINAL EXERCISE OF THIS WORKBOOK. CONGRATULATIONS!

For your last challenge, you'll have to reflect, truly thinking about how you think learning cursive will help you. On the lines provided on the next page, you'll write out these thoughts. Once you finish these final paragraphs, you will be ready to receive your special certificate! Think about the different ways cursive can be useful, such as helping you write faster, making your writing look neat, or connecting with older styles of writing. Once you complete this paragraph, you will be ready to receive your Cursive Pro certificate!

CURSIVE REFLECTION

Cursive Pro

This certificate is presented to

WITNESS SIGNATURE

About Applesauce Press

Good ideas ripen with time. From seed to harvest, Applesauce Press crafts books with beautiful designs, creative formats, and kid-friendly information on a variety of fascinating topics. Like our parent company, Cider Mill Press Book Publishers, our press bears fruit twice a year, publishing a new crop of titles each spring and fall.

"WHERE GOOD BOOKS ARE READY FOR PRESS"
501 NELSON PLACE
NASHVILLE, TENNESSEE 37214

CIDERMILLPRESS.COM